So You Want to be a Grassroots Referee?

by Reg Wilson

© Copyright Richard Wood 2016

All views shared in this book are the views of Reg Wilson only. Reg Wilson does not represent the views of the FA, UEFA, FIFA or any other football governing body.

Cover Design by GoOnWrite.com

For Reg Wilson's football blog visit www.redcardranting.com

Reg Wilson

This book is dedicated to all those full time referees who carry out their jobs brilliantly under huge pressure.

Contents

Introduction 8
About Me 9
Your Equipment 11
Dealing with Abuse and Dissent 14
Going for Promotion 20
Managing Your Club Assistants 22
Being an Assistant 23
Dealing with Mistakes 26
Report Writing and Hearings 28
Being Proactive and Selling Your Decision 30
Final Words 33

Introduction

So, you've decided to become a referee! You have completed the course, passed the test, and ordered your kit. Now what?

Now you are going to have to go out there and control 22 passionate players with 2 cards and whistle.

This book isn't a how-to on refereeing, nor is it a substitute for guidance from the FA that you will receive from your mentor and/or referee development officer. This book is simply a guide on what to expect when you start refereeing, and a sharing of some advice.

What equipment do I need for my first match? What happens when I get abuse? What level of dissent is okay? What happens if I want to go for promotion? What about when I am asked to be an assistant referee? How do I write a red card report?

And, most importantly, how do I deal with making a mistake?

I will attempt to answer these questions from my experience of seven years as a grassroots referee in various counties. I will offer you some thoughts and direction on how to deal with these different situations and issues, all of which you will probably face.

This is my guide on how to be a grassroots referee.

About Me

I started refereeing in 2009 in Cheltenham. I also officiated in Staffordshire and Birmingham in my time at University, before settling in my current county. I grew up watching football on television with my Dad and older brother. I reached 18 and my passion for football really started to grow – but I knew, with my complete lack of coordination and footballing ability, that I stood no chance of becoming a football player. But, maybe I could make it as a football referee?

This is me as fourth official at an under-13 cup final in my first season as a level 7 referee. I have come a long way since then. I am now a level 5 referee, hopefully on track to becoming a level 4, which will give me the opportunity to potentially start officiating on semi-professional football.

I was even asked to officiate on two cup finals as assistant referee this season, which was a great honour.

Here is me giving an offside decision on one of those finals!

Your equipment

You will need to get a referee kit. The requirements for this change slightly every few seasons, but at the time of going to print, it is recommended that you have little to no white on your kit. You can get a relatively cheap referee kit on Amazon, but I would highly recommend using A&H to buy your kit. They will provide you with a sustainable, professional kit, that you can buy with your FA's badge already on it; which is often a requirement of your FA.

Remember – the moment you arrive at the ground you are being watched. Players and Managers are unconsciously making an impression of you. If you show up in a cheap, self-branded kit, compared to a professional looking Nike or Umbro kit, consider what impression you may be giving.

You will also need a whistle. You can get many different types of whistle, but I would highly recommend either a FOX 40 or Acme Thunder. Again, you can get these from A&H or other sites such as Amazon. Other whistles will be fine, but these two whistles have a far more professional and assertive sound.

You will need to get a referee's pad with some game sheets. Often these game sheets come with the pad, but if not, you can buy some on A&H. I often use blank sheets of paper instead of the template given so I don't have to follow their prescribed format.

With the pad, you should get a red and yellow card – do not forget these! You don't want to face a violent conduct incident without a red card to produce.

When producing a red or yellow card, you can take one from the back of your referee's pad and record the player's information on your game sheet; I even know some referees who write the full team sheet into their pad to record bookings and dismissals. Personally, I keep my red and yellow cards in my short pockets as this enables me to be able to produce them quickly. I then write the player's shirt number and kit colour on the back of the card, and use the team sheets to look up their name later. Saying this, the FA advise you to take a player's name when you book or dismiss them, as this prevents problems such as a team sheet being undreadable.

Of course, if your league doesn't do team sheets, as is often the case with youth leagues, you will need to get the player's name and write this down when you produce a card. Often this is better for a pad. Ultimately, it is up to you to find your best procedure.

A coin. You can buy special FA coins, but personally I use a 2p coin. I have forgotten it once or twice and had to get them to guess which whistle my hand is in instead; but again, think about what impression you want to give, and whether forgetting your coin for the toss is the best first impression.

You will need small pencils to record match information on your pad and/or cards. You can get a big pack of these fairly cheaply.

You will need to make sure you have some flags ready for your club assistants. These can too be bought easily from A&H and Amazon.

A watch with a stopwatch. You might want to have two, so you can stop one in order to time breaks in play.

Football boots with studs. Make sure you get the right football boots for your feet, as poorly fitting football boots can lead to infected toes – and this is not a great reason to be out injured! You may also want to make sure you have some molds in case it is a particularly hard surface, or if you happen to referee a team that plays on AstroTurf.

Boot cleaner is optional – but if you decide to go for promotion it is a good idea, as I have known some assessors to mark referees down for the presentation of their boots.

So, to summarize, this is the list of what you need:
- Kit, with t-shirt, shorts and socks. A thermal top is optional, but if you do get one for those wintery games, make sure it is the same colour as your kit.
- Whistle
- Referee's pad with match sheets
- Red and yellow cards
- A coin
- Pencils
- Football boots and moulds
- Assistant Flags
- Watch

Dealing with Abuse and Dissent

Unfortunately, there is no way around it. You will get abuse. It is part of the job, as it is for most authority figures. Ask any police officer, teacher, traffic warden, boss – they will have all gotten some form of abuse at some point.

The FA have done great work in reducing this. Their Respect campaign has eradicated a lot of the abuse that we, as officials, face. Unfortunately, you can only do so much. We should be grateful that we do have such passionate players and spectators to referee; but with passion, comes bias and frustration that can often manifest itself against the referee.

I once had a conversation with a referee that officiates on the Football League who gave me some advice that really helped me. He told me that, in most games, he will get abuse; and he just has to accept it.

It's awful to think that we should have to accept and come to terms with getting abuse, I know. But if you can go into a game knowing and accepting that there will be some, it makes it a lot easier to deal with.

And so what? What are they going to say to you that actually means anything?

"That was shit, ref." Well actually, no it wasn't, as you evidently don't know how I was applying the laws then.

"Who's the bastard in the black?" Me. And my parents were married when I was born.

"The referee's a wanker." Well, yes, on occasion, but haven't we all done that?

Ultimately, the only time abuse will actually bother me, is if I have genuinely made a mistake and I think they may be right. And you will make mistakes, especially in your first season, and you will get quite a lot of stick for it. But once you've persevered and you have experience behind you, it then becomes very rare that they actually are right. Most of the time someone gives you abuse it's because they don't actually know what they are talking about.

I once heard a commentator say "there are 3 of them offside, why isn't he flagging?" when the ball was in the opposite half. I mean, if commentators talk such rubbish, it's going to leave an impression on the players we referee at grassroots level. So, as long as you know you got the decision right, what does it matter about what others say?

Of course, you should always try and sell your decisions as best as you can and there are ways of doing this (see later chapter). But there are some decisions, and even some games, where you will not please everyone. If you officiate in a game between rivals or a cup final, it is unlikely all players are going to be happy with you at the end, no matter how amazing you are.

It is then ultimately up to you where your tolerance level is. You have the right to have a word with a player, book them for either dissent or adopting an aggressive attitude, or dismiss them for foul and abusive language. You need to decide what you are, and are not, going to accept – and stick with it.

Saying that, I haven't always dealt with abuse and dissent in the correct way. Below are two incidents where I have gotten abuse at grassroots level and how I dealt with it.

1/ A mother hurling abuse at my club assistant
Youth games will most likely see you receive more dissent than adult male games – mostly from the parents! This was an incident where my club assistant was doing an excellent job, yet a Mother from the opposition's team didn't agree. This was an under-16 game where I'd already sent one child off for foul and abusive language toward me.

I went over and warned her that she needed to leave my assistant alone. I didn't just say "leave him alone," I was clear and confident in where I wanted her to go and what I wanted her to do. "I need you to return to the other side of the pitch so you won't be tempted to involve yourself in my assistant."

She did, however, continue. I went over again and told her that if she didn't return to her team's side of the pitch and leave the assistant alone, I would abandon the game and it would all be her fault. She stayed away from him then.

As well as this worked, I think you need to be careful with what threat you give; I needed to be ready to follow through and abandon the game if she didn't then do as asked. Fortunately, I didn't have to face that problem. A better consequence I could have used is reporting her club to the FA for failing to control their spectators, which I ended up doing anyway.

2/ The man behind me at a cup final
I was the assistant referee at a cup final and I had a large amount of spectators behind me. There was a key match decision that involve me deciding on whether the ball had crossed the line for a goal. A spectator didn't like my decision. He stood behind the barrier, around 3 yards behind me, shouting "eh, lino, lino, you saw that, you saw that you cheating c**t!"

In the end, I turned around and told him to shut up. This was a lesson learnt. I got an aggressive reply of "you don't want to tell me to shut up." I wasn't scared or intimidated, more frustrated with myself that I had opened up communication with him.

If you react to spectators, they will know that you are listening. Even if a spectator asks you much time is left, a perfectly innocent question, think about what this could entail. If you respond to that, when the spectator starts reacting to a decision they don't like, they will likely persist. I know it's hard, almost impossible sometimes, but you must not react.

If you need to, report the club afterwards; as they are the ones who should be controlling such abuse.

Foul and Abusive Language
As I have pointed out, there are multiple laws of the game you can use to react to dissent and abuse from players. You can give a yellow card for 'dissent' or 'adopting an aggressive attitude.' Likewise, you can produce a red card for 'foul and abusive language or gestures.'

Just make sure in these situations that you are not reacting emotionally and you have thought through your decision with a rational mind. Personally, I have a limit as to what I will accept. I have had a player call me a 'cheating c**t.' The 'c**t' part of that sentence part seem like the most offensive word. But to me, it isn't. Calling me a 'cheat' completely undermines and offends the job I am performing. I produced a red card to that player for that reason.

Likewise, if a player says "that was shit, ref," you can justify it within the law to produce a red. But would that help your match control? If you set a precedent for what will happen when someone says that, you will have to be consistent with it throughout. Think with a rational mind what would be the best decision.

Depending upon how heated the match is, often referees suggest going through the following steps with someone who giving you too much stick:
- A quiet word of warning
- A public word of warning with their captain
- Then a booking

Although, if the dissent was starting to get aggressive and the match heated, you might decide to produce on far earlier. Ultimately, it is up to you to decide what you will accept and what you won't.

Often, things are said in the heat of the moment. In my first season, I once had a manager storm up to me after the game and say he was going to see to it that I never referee a game again. Seven years later, he hasn't done a very good job.

Remember – none of these comments you get will reflect on your ability to referee. They will usually be spoken by biased people with little knowledge of the laws of the game. Even the pundits and commentators on television frequently get it wrong. If you know you got the decision is correct and sold it as best as you can, then you can be confident in yourself whatever anyone says to you.

Going for Promotion

After you've finished your first season and you find you are enjoying it, you may well want to go for promotion. This is a brilliant idea, mostly as it means an FA assessor will come watch you and give you feedback, which really helps in your development as a referee.

As I write this the level system may be changing, so you will need to speak to your Referee Development Officer about the levels.

What is required for each promotion varies with different county FAs, but this is what most promotions will require:

- A written test on the laws of the game
- A minimum amount of games you will need to officiate on. Keep a record of these, as you may need to submit a list of games you have done come the end of the promotion campaign.
- A small amount of games as assistant referee
- A minimum amount of assessments. Make sure you send your games to your FA's assessment officer every month to ensure you get enough assessments.
- Some FAs take into account club marks, some don't. Don't get to hung up on this, as most leagues have a policy that if a club gives a mark lower than a certain number, they have to submit a report as to why; to which most clubs can't be bothered. I have had numerous clubs say they are going to 'complain' about me and it has never hindered my progress!
- As you climb further up the levels, you may need to do a fitness test.

Your County FA's Referee Development Officer will be able to tell you more about what is required for promotion with your FA. Even if you aren't going to promotion, it is a good idea to get to know this person, as they are crucial to your development as a referee.

Managing Your Club Assistants

Club assistants can be an amazing help or an antagonizing hindrance. Although clubs may swap their club assistants during the game, make sure that when you get your first club assistants before kick-off you still make clear to them what you expect. For me, I normally include the following:
- I only want offsides and ball in and out of play; no fouls
- If I overrule you, I'm sorry
- If anyone is giving you too much stick, wave the flag and bring me over

They should be there to help you, but you will inevitably get assistants who are either biased or incompetent. There is little advice I can give you in dealing with them, as it comes down to your call in particular decisions.

Make sure they are running the line for their own defense, so if they are more interested in the cigarette in their mouth and the woman they're chatting up behind them and fail to give a crucial offside, it will only be at the cost of his own team.

Often, the main issue with club assistants is that they don't know the laws of the game, meaning they may, for example, flag someone for offside who never actually interfered in play. It is up to you whether you go with them or shout "flag down" and explain the decision to the captain in the next stoppage in play.

Being an Assistant

You will, sooner or later, get to the point where you will assistant referee a match. As you climb up the levels, you will probably find yourself doing more and more. It is different to being a referee in that it's far more technical; you are mostly looking for offsides and ball in/out of play, which lack the subjectivity of interpreting a foul (although as an assistant, you will still of course need to give fouls within your 'area' of the pitch).

This would probably be a good point to remind you of the various flag signals you will need to use as an assistant referee.

Offside – lift your flag up until it is completely horizontal. Once the referee has blown for the free kick, lower your flag to indicate where the free kick is to be taken. Have it pointed directly in front of your chest if the kick is to be taken half way between you and the opposite side of the pitch, pointed downwards if the kick is closer to you and pointed upwards if it is on the far side.

Throw In – lift the flag diagonally upwards to your side, indicating which team's throw in it is by pointing it in the direction in which that team is attacking.

Foul / Free Kick – wave your flag above your head, changing the length of time in which you wave it according to the severity of the foul, before then pointing in the direction in which the side you have given the foul for is attacking, much like you would a throw in.

Goal kick – point the flag directly in front of your chest.

Corner Kick – point the flag diagonally downwards at the corner flag.

Being an assistant referee is often a brilliant opportunity to learn from a referee who is more experienced than you. There may be things you see them do that you will want to use for your refereeing. Likewise, there may be things you see the referee do that you think aren't particularly fitting to your style of officiating.

An example of something I have taken from a referee is their communication with players over advantage. When he wanted to see where play went after the foul to see if there was an advantage, but wanted to make sure the players knew he had seen the foul, he would put the whistle beside his mouth and shout "I've seen it, I've seen it." If there was no advantage, he'd then reply "no advantage, bring it back" or "advantage, play on" if there was. I now use this every game and find it works brilliantly.

I have worked with some brilliant referees as an assistant, but as with every job, you will occasionally come across people that don't impress you so much. I once ran the line for a referee who was incredibly arrogant, running around with his collar up and shouting on every foul "no, you've seen too much premier league football, that's not a foul" (he was rather old-fashioned.) He told us, as assistants, not to give any fouls. As a player was down injured, he paced back and forth next to him droning on about why it wasn't a foul. He helped my development as a referee greatly by showing me exactly the kind of referee I don't want to be.

Your referee will most likely give you a pre-match talk about what they expect in various scenarios. The main thing is to make sure you listen and take on board what they want and ask any questions about what you aren't certain of.

For me, the two hardest parts of being an assistant is checking I am in line with the last defender whilst also checking for throw ins and fouls, as well as remembering which way each team are shooting. I concentrate a lot on these things as I run the line as a result and they act as my own personal development points.

Normally, out of the two Assistant Referees, one will be the Senior Assistant. This means that you will run the line next to the benches. At the level you are officiating it is very unlikely you will have a fourth official, which means that if you are Senior Assistant, it will be your job to manage the benches. It is ultimately up to you and your referee how you choose to manage them. The general rules are that only two people can stand at any one time, there is a limit of three non-players and five substitutes and all people in the benches must be named on the team sheet; although this changes, according to your particular league rules. You and your referee need to decide how strict you are going to be with this; ultimately this will likely be something your referee will go over in pre-match. Personally, I tend to become stricter should the benches be becoming more tense and/or aggressive.

Dealing with Mistakes

We are all human. As humans, we inevitably make mistakes. Even Premier League officials at the top of their game will occasionally get a decision wrong. In my first two seasons, I had many sleepless nights I spent staring at the ceiling following a game, going over decisions again and again.

Be proactive about it. Think about the mistake rationally. Did you have the right position? Were you up with play? Did you not sell it well? Whatever the reason, learn from it and make sure you are better placed for when another incident like it occurs. If you need to, talk to the Referee Development Officer at your FA about it; they are there to support you and help your development and may help you to pick it apart and figure out what went wrong.

Dealing with the mistake is all about the mind set you take.

If you make a mistake you will often have players coming up to you and accusing you of costing them the game, because of that one mistake. Let's think about this for a moment. Count up in your mind – how many times did that player misplace a pass? Miss a shot? Get a tackle wrong? Have a poor first touch? They will have made far more mistakes than you which are likely to have cost them the game.

Try setting yourself a time limit for how long you are allowed to be angry about having a bad game. I normally give myself until 8pm that night. If I had an awful game, I am only allowed to be miserable and angry about it until 8 that evening. I will have gotten my reports done by then so I can forget about it and I will move on.

Likewise, if you had a really good game, give yourself until 8pm to be smug about it. Carrying arrogance or lack of confidence into a game will not help you; you need to be focussed in the next match, not thinking back to the previous game and hoping you don't screw up again.

In your first season, possibly even your second season, there's no way around it; you will make lots of mistakes. You're new and are learning. No one gets it right straight away. Unfortunately, players won't see it that way and will be less than forgiving to new referees.

In these cases, remember to use it for your development. There are many things I do now, things I look for and decisions I make, that I do as a result of what I learnt in my first two seasons. The experience of making that mistake and learning from it has been invaluable. Without those mistakes, I wouldn't be a good referee now.

Report Writing and Hearings

You will need to write reports for all of your red cards and any incidents where you report a club. Some leagues also require you to write a report on each game. The main thing to remember with report writing and hearings is to only report the facts. Leave your emotional involvement and your personal feelings out of it and ensure that you only report what happened.

For example, here is an example of a poorly written report:

After badgering me for the whole match, this player came up to me and followed me around. He kept on giving me grief, then he told me I'm a "fucking idiot." I got very annoyed, made everyone stop and showed him the red card, shaking my head at him.

There is a lot of unneeded information in there. Let's think about what the facts are and what needs to be reported. Whilst the player may have been annoying to the referee the whole match, the report is focussing on the isolated incident around the red card, not what's happened before. Again, saying that you got annoyed and shook your head, whilst it clearly shows the frustration the referee may be feeling whilst writing the report, isn't particularly relevant.

This is how I would have written the report:

The player ran toward me and told me that I was a 'fucking idiot.' I blew my whistle to stop the game, produced the red card, and the player left the field of play.

Should you ever need to go to a hearing over something you have written in your report, you will need still need to remember to just report the facts. I had to go to a hearing after I sent a boy of in an under 17 game for assaulting me.

I was unsure about whether or not to include this incident in this book, as I did not want to put you off what is a hugely enjoyable past time. So I do wish to point out that an incident like this is rare. The FA couldn't have been more supportive about the situation; as soon as I sent in the report, I had three different people from the FA call me to check that I was okay. Should I have wanted to go to the police for assault, they would have fully supported me. Whilst this made me stop refereeing for a few months the following season, I returned and came back better than ever, learning from experience. Please do not let my recollection of this put you off pursuing what you are passionate about.

In the game in question, I gave an awful penalty decision, which ultimately led to this incident. In the hearing, the manager of the under-17 team attempted a defamation of my character by using this. He cited this and various other incidents in the match to convince the board at the hearing that I didn't see things in the same way as other people. This was, of course, irrelevant, as the boy in question had assaulted me; which had nothing to do with how I 'saw things.' It was really hard for me to just report the facts and not retaliate in my testimony. As it was, I managed to stay emotionally uninvolved and I testified about what happened using just the facts. In the end, I came across far better than the manager and the repercussions for the player in question were rightfully harsh.

Being Proactive and Selling Your Decision

Good refereeing is about being proactive and selling your decisions. In this section I am going to look at what I mean by this and some ways that you can be proactive in your refereeing.

Being proactive means looking for possible problems before they come up. When you make a mistake in your refereeing, you will need to look at that mistake and decide what you can do to prevent it from happening next time.

The first point of being proactive is your pre-match pitch inspection. Look for anything that may cause you problems in the match and consider how you can be proactive in dealing with it.

For example, is the penalty spot clearly marked? If it isn't, I will warn the captains before I do the coin toss that there are no penalty marks, so in case of the penalty, I will walk 10 yards from the goal line to indicate where the penalty need to be taken from.

Are the nets pegged down well? Imagine if the side of the net isn't pegged down properly and the ball fires through it during the game and both sides contest whether it is a goal; could you prevent that by asking the home team to peg down the gap?

Your talk to the captains before the coin toss will be useful in being proactive; just remember that whatever you say to the captains, you will need to follow through on. In my second season, I decided that any abuse toward me would be met with a red card, so I warned the captains about this; meaning that when I gave a red card for foul and abusive language, the captain's reaction was "well he did warn us." I don't say this anymore, however, as I don't want to be committed to giving a red card for every time a player swears in my direction.

If you get a confrontation during the game, consider what you could have done to prevent it. I was fourth official on a cup final and I saw a foul a few yards from me that the referee didn't give. The player looked to the ref, saw it wasn't given, so went for the other player instead, meaning a mass confrontation broke out. The referee could have prevented this by seeing that tension was rising, giving a harsh free kick against one of those two players and talking to them together about calming down.

When a defender is running after a sprinting attacker, or jumping for the ball, I will shout "hands down!" This simply warns them that if they don't stop grappling at the other player with their hands, I will give a foul. This means when I give the foul, no one is arguing with me as I have sold the decision well.

Selling your decisions comes with experience and being proactive, although there are some things you can do straight from the beginning to ensure you sell your decisions:

- Be confident. If you put your hand up for a throw in or a foul, make sure it is a strong, confident hand signal, not a limp hand up.
- It's your decision as to when to be quick in giving a decision and when to take your time; either can be used to sell the decision. You may want to blow the whistle then slowly move your arm to point, or you may want to make a quick decision and wave away the protests.
- Be next to the foul when you blow the whistle. So if you are ten yards away, get next to the foul, so people will see that you are closer to the incident than them.
- Your position. Make sure your view is unobstructed and the correct distance away.

Something I am yet to mention is that you need to be proactive and responsible with your use of social media. Be careful about posting any statuses or comments about a match you've taken part in, a team you have refereed or anything else that could bring your position into disrepute. I have a blog in which I write about football, and use Facebook and Twitter I use to promote this – but I am very careful as to what I post, and do so under a pseudonym (Reg Wilson is not my real name!) I will only use the blog to explain decisions, not criticise, as I do not wish to upset anybody at the FA that may read it.

Even if your accounts are on private, you may have a referee or FA associate you are friends with who will see what you post; so be careful.

Final Words

So, there you have it. You are about to embark upon a brilliant hobby and potential career. Whether you just wanted to learn a bit more about it, have a run around on a Saturday morning or have ambition to referee in the Premier League, you have started your path on an exciting journey.

I didn't write this book with the intention of giving you a long, complicated, word-filled guide on how to referee. I wrote it with the intention of giving you a small book I know would have helped me when I first started.

If you would like to get in contact, or let me know what other questions you would have liked answered, please visit my blog at www.redcardranting.com

Remember to use the FA and your colleague's support, as that is crucial to your perseverance and development.

But most of all, make sure to enjoy it! And hopefully I will see you on the pitch one day.

Appendix

In order to help you with your first few refereeing fixtures, I have come up with some checklists. These are guidelines which will hopefully ensure that you manage to cover everything as you get used to your pre-match routine.

Appendix 1 Equipment Checklist

Before you leave for your first fixture, make sure you have the following:

	Kit: shorts, socks and jersey
	Whistle
	Assistant flags
	Referee pad with match sheets
	Red and yellow cards
	Coin
	Pencils
	Football boots and moulds
	Stopwatch

Appendix 2

Your pre-match checklist:

	Arrive at least 30 minutes before kick off
	Pitch inspection; check markings, goal nets and for any unwanted items on the ground
	Warm up
	If your league does team sheets, collect them, ensuring names and shirt numbers are clearly stated
	Check you have all you need with you: whistle, coin, cards, match pad, pencil and watch.
	Give assistant flags to your club assistants and ensure they understand what you require from them
	Two minutes before kick-off, blow your whistle to bring the captains in, do the coin toss and give your captain talk

Appendix 3

When the match has finished:

	Check you have the names of any bookings or dismissals you have given
	Collect your money
	Send in any bookings or dismissals as soon as you arrive home

Then be proud that you have completed your first match as a referee!

For Reg Wilson's football blog, please visit and subscribe to:

www.redcardranting.com

Reg Wilson

Printed in Great Britain
by Amazon